Also by Guichard Cadet

LoneWolf's Cry
0-9647635-0-8; Feb. 1996

The Masks of Flipside
0-9647635-4-0; May 1998

The Canon of Loose Canons
0-9718191-2-2; July 2002

Other La Caille Nous titles

Separate but Equal
0-9718191-4-9; Sept. 2002

Backfield in Motion
0-9718191-3-0; Aug. 2002

When He Calls
0-9647635-9-1; June 2002

Father's Footsteps
0-9718191-1-4; June 2002

Water in a Broken Glass
0-9647635-7-5; Sept. 2000

When You Look At Me
0-9647635-6-7; June 2000

Temples
0-9647635-5-9; Feb. 1999

Party Ain't Over Yet!
0-9647635-3-2; March 1997

The A# Blu's
0-9647635-2-4; Sept. 1996

My Baby's Father
0-9647635-8-3; April 2001 (revd.)

bard from par taken

episodes of a haimeri poetic lifetime
volume II

bard from par taken

episodes of a haimeri poetic lifetime
volume II

Guichard Cadet

La Caille Nous

Edited by: Cassandra Cantave & Marie Michael
Cover Design: Shane Hudalla

Cadet, Guichard, 1968-
    Bard from par taken / Guichard Cadet.
        p. cm. – (Episodes of a Haimeri poetic lifetime; v.2)
        ISBN 0-9718191-0-6 (pbk. :alk. Paper)

PS3553.A31345 B37 2002
811'.54—dc21   2002023049

La Caille Nous Publishing Company, Inc.
PO Box 1004
Riverdale, MD 20738
www.lcnpub.com

Media & Distribution
328 Flatbush Avenue, Suite 240
Brooklyn, NY 11238
212-726-1293

dedicated to Earl, Folson, Randy, my brothers in Kappa, and all men who understand that life gives us one truth and many words to express it.

Smile for me!

Acknowledgments:

Randolph Morton for stepping into the company, "lifting boxes" and truly providing the "help" that so many have offered.

Marie Michael for her editorial work on this volume and my upcoming fiction, *The Canon of Loose Cannons*, and for the evolving friendship.

Charmaine Bennett, my love, for the countless hours we spend together helping each other realize our dreams, our life.

prologue

Letter from the Commissioner: an interpretation

This brings up the past
because it starts so simply

> *Dear SlowFoot,*
> *"An old man people ask what you did with your life:*
> *I hated LL and carried a big knife." - LL Cool J*

Mending Wings doesn't understand anger,
neither side, the sadness nor the madness.
To know that's who we are, I am
yet he wants to separate the dream from the reality.

To believe or try to explain that there is this divider,
as he fancies himself, wearing the tattered garbs.
So on the Council of Elders, he sits in the middle,
Wisdom's Chair. He sees only the past,
as compartments. Draws a line to show

Where reality ended. Where the dream started
to the wise it is a simple thing, so many listen
including me. I, who has also been crowned a Wise,
for the knowledge I possess makes me a realist

> *"that's why some prefer rice*
> *and others, pasta."*

Laugh is all I could do, recalling why he eats
his rice undercooked, to separate the dream

can't fathom that dreams are within us.

> bard from par taken <

To one day slit the throat, fully consume
the boiling pit in which we swim.

Swam!! Oh yes, I remember the past.
Well not really! I only say that,
As not to let them jump
to the conclusion. That I have switched sides

"to make the peace, I have signed
a letter of intent on your behalf."

The audacity to equate my singularity
with the extremists, the loners who have taken a vow of solidarity,
marrying warring houses after seeing my fires extinguish,
to either bat lefty or marry, thus the understanding.

For or Against! Mending Wings doesn't get it,
to have crowned LoneWolf a wise,
see him sit at the far side of the table:
FLIPSIDE.

Sorry I went against you! I only

Did it to break the line, they all said
fearing the suffix *ing,* perpetual motion

against this bridge with those who have never walked

The path is deadly! Yes, and
I believe in reincarnation. So cremate me;

These old ideas. Of unity,

> guichard cadet <

I'd rather walk half-circle
to reach LoneWolf, the other side,
than meet Mending Wings in the middle,
Call me bitter, crazy…but I know
why he conjugates his verbs: compartments.

> *"The suffix ed ended the war. Your followers flipped*
> *it to a prefix- educate- then mixed it with an ing!"*

Ingenious. How they started the past again,
it made me smile, the fraction:
a fanatical faction following my lead,
albeit, clandestinely, to sit at the table and break bread.
All the while fracturing this truce some call a Peace.

Crime! Pride! War!
We never had a choice. Great works of literature
do not contain the word OR.
and AND was never meant as a divider
yet you question my authority.

Strike the last line for it is neither

> *"Ball or Strike! We are playing*
> *One-Pitch because you should have never been barred."*

That's your shame! Yours,

I gambled the house would fall apart
Without me, they survived, as a shadow
of themselves, against themselves

> bard from par taken <

With my back to the wall, I can't shoot
My followers are in front of me. I fear them
with their backs turned
because they weren't there when I left
yet they know my name, have read my book

They can only live
If I swing at this pitch.
Mending Wings wins either way,
and that's why he sits in the middle.

<>

Cigar & Rosé: The Stains of My Past

I am not going to make the same mistake again. This time I will only be a ceremonial user, unlike the first time, when Art became my lover. She, a canvas, a blank page, clay or whatever she chose to be with others. But, for me she was Rosé.

On a sunny day, out of bambu, I cut open a cigar, the smoke filled my lungs, and she wrapped herself around me. Snake, I once thought Art to be because I got caught up in her, and ended up an Artist.

No major stylistic changes in terms of fashion, but our being had morphed. Cute couple we were but never in public. Some saw us as rebels, misfits, so we chose to remain behind closed doors. Solitude.

A state in which I realized that I was writing to live, locking myself up in a cage, staying alone or only with Art, which in the end became synonymous.

II

Now, I no longer cut open cigars. Expensive ones don't need that, but after forty, I began to cough smoke, hours and days after smoking. I had been polluted and realized so was my Art. Then I had to question which one of us was the Snake, trying to control the other, locking allegiance as a result of time and repetition.

Then I recalled our innocence. We first me in a group then became loners within the group, learning to function within it yet we were so far apart, recalling and enjoying the good life, when I was alone with Rosé, my most loved.

> bard from par taken <

I will always cherish the occasional tryst, the kiss after eating
Mexican, a week after I made your acquaintance. You looked so
lovely that day, draped in purple and white. Your eyes, cloudy. The
smoke; the whispers of bards could be heard. We were in public.
Your touch was subtle, yet the implication was clear.

Could you have a quickie before class? If so, can I lick because
your period comes in two days. You asked, "Cigar, could I turn
myself into you; have permission to lock my soul into your lungs?"

From then, I felt like I was sailing on our dreamboat, drinking rosé
and smoking a cigar, with my rod baiting fish. A dark fog had
enveloped me. I had no peripheral vision. All I could see and sense
was the tunnel. So you left!!

III
Yes! It was that deep, that new but only because I had forgotten to
be an Artist, I had to live to write, to burn in the fire, have new
experiences.

Why did I become celibate, acting as if I was a kid who refuses to
ride again because he fell off while riding a cycle that left him under
a cruising car?

When I saw that you were fine without me, I realized that I also did
not need you. I had lost my tongue yet I babbled...cackled at the
midnight hour that it was necessary for an artist to be alone.

But you asked, "Who needs an artist if all he does is bring to life a
mental state that can only exist physically?" Reality was not high
enough for me and it was never Art's agenda.

> guichard cadet <

Couldn't I not see her devotion? The time she spent nurturing my inner soul could only be represented properly by the aura given by her outer shell.

<>

prelude to lonely hearts & bitterness

Love's Cup

In youth, there's always beauty.

even if the bowl is not filled to the rim
and future prospects seem grim,
A smile is present.

Whether the smile of adoration
        or ignorance, it looms bright,
        yet not daunting.

The open door of youth invites,
        with threshold uncrossed
        and darkness unseen.

There is carelessness,
a stumbling,
and the many more chances ahead.

<Ahead, there is a road>
        for as many who wish to come
        and share in the warmth,
        the willingness to pass the cup.

Hand in hand,
        in the circle of lines parallel,
        perpendicular, and North and South;
        lines where East meets West.

At points center,
        on the graph

> bard from par taken <

where each grafts an existence,
we take a stance.

On the happy,
hard times
of rays that exceed
and those who have bled.

For us to get far,
sacrifices have to be made.
But let's not part,
even if we take.

Hunger must be combated;
Youth must quench.

In order for the sun to shine,
brightly, mercifully,
and daily,
We must agree.

<>

Obsession

Never takes one day but only hurts one way.
Ever stop for a moment and realize you
Don't play mind games for fear her attention may sway.
Even when you're telling the truth, you dare not look into her eyes.
No time for others, 'cause you were admiring this creation.
In control of everything important, except for the situation.
At last, after many, many weeks, you named it- Infatuation.

Indescribable

A slightly-wet brush stroking a canvas
     with its dark-maroon coating
     intruding
     with permission, if I may
     be so polite in spite of vanity
     be allowed to bask in the sun
     near the rainbow
     where all colors are jovial, radiant
     bursts of togetherness
     of light eyes in the dark
     blankets on the grass
     happiness under the sky that stores
     richness in our hearts.
Not clear enough!
     You're pillow while we talk
     a form of security
     that blankets
     my every turn & consideration.
     with permission, if I may
     be so forward in spite of my shyness
     be trusted to secure the treasures
     of your heart where all feelings are acceptable
     even harsh ones.
More definition!
     Perfectly woven spiral
     thrown
     caught by one who was asked
     "Little girl, you want some candy?"
     Pepper
     meant to spice

> guichard cadet <

Liquor
each drop intoxicating
breath
to the last. Do we part?
migrate like birds
change like seasons.
Relate it to something concrete!
A sign of vulnerability
Enters as you appear
I stop making sense
Oh my gosh – I start sounding funny because
U are *********
FORGET IT!

<>

Waterfalls

Honestly. The way I saw it
was weird.
Ducking punches,
cold stares flashing in the darkness
the strobe light disguising my sadness

The men grabbing at you
as if you were the last piece of cold chicken;
not truly fighting one another,
more like mocking, hiding their true intentions.

Honestly. Do I love you?
The way I saw it
made me. Think
of how it felt
being one of the men
picking at you
starving for recognition,
realizing that you were alive-
a worm.

So I retreated,
took a good look around
and saw the other major players:
Insecure and Clown.
Honestly.

I concluded that you were a snake,
a parasite that forged
a symbiotic relation with Eve.

17

> guichard cadet <

Even though the book was Revelation,

The major players needed
to control you

in public. You're scared
because you can't show
your true colors: green
a venom spewing out of a robotic shell

piece.
This together and
all the things I saw

brought me to my childhood.
Little Rascals hounding Darla
because Alfalfa's dead, for
no one wants to sing that song,
sway from the contingency;
No one!

Honestly. Together we are
more vulnerable than
apart.
I got your back;
only because last night a DJ
saved my life

As I reached for a seat,
thinking the music would stop,
he spun a vicious mix, a clue-
"Don't go chasing waterfalls…"

Chivalry's Return

Now that I'm older
I smile much more
because I find it funny
that with all the independence you proclaim,
you stand still

At the edge, after the first step
where love turns into a sewery moat,
you wait

for me to throw down my jacket,
and help you over,
serve as a life preserver,
that difficult knot, you can't swim

only because you refuse
to try
to see. if I'll rescue you

<>

Antidote

Layers of skin,
serving as a shell,

If uncovered, peeled
off the other men in your life

You'll find me.
if you're bold

Keep searching until you reach
the mirror, my soul

You will then see
whether it's shame or fancy

Mirrors may obscure the shape,
but they don't hide you.

<>

African Features

Gentle,
Cool as the breeze
Who seizes
The core,
the mantle,
and the crust.

Bold.
As a bone plucked well,
Let me tell

Of round
brown eyes
shapely thighs,
cheeks that blush
brighter than a cig's butt,
and tongue
so long, it nearly brought me

To the next episode.

The drinks were done.
We were alone;
we smiled a mild
then left it at that.

Warm as it may sound,
It didn't last a day.

Less than twenty-four

21

More than a year.

Those features, like short stories
do not last
but are first
because they teach us:
      Only the middle is bound.

<>

An Eternal Lesson

She was
Young, Willing & Either
And taught me
> Not to respect
> one who jets
> from oppression
> then comes back thinking
> "the course will be easier this time"

She was
phat
but I was living too
careless,
irresponsible
and dry.

The funds weren't flowing
but I was still
flooding the market.

Like two birds,
we flew as if the air
we breathed
couldn't lead.

To our death

Ears didn't see,
didn't heed.
(Didn't he

23

do the deed?)
Over there and over
in Mass
Media Awareness:

It was a struggle
between religion, philosophy
and sexuality, as in biology.

In school, I failed chemistry
until I saw her though she was
a captive in na'ivity

Her upbringing told her no,
Her girlfriend laid that
to rest with another,
we formed a quadrilateral
with no right angles.

Later I learned:
The virgin had a son,
Space! was the father
Society? or the
Shapeless Shadow
who stumbled
over the grave of his soul.

Her name for me: Socrates
stands tall
but please do not tale
of me,
If you will not

> bard from par taken <

tell

Of All.
who have caught the call

Don't drop the stones of nativity unless
Your name is embedded on their hearts.

<>

Tap-Tapping

Tap Tapping into my soul
searching for the shivers aboard;
calm and collected I may not seem
but I'll never lose my cool

I may wake with sweat on my body
but I'll never swap spit with a child;
old as the yellowing snow,
young and refresh as the morning sun

        Tap-Tapping into my soul
        drawing me to be near you
Your soft breath on my nape,
your questioning eyes on my lips;
If I smile for you,
would that be too much
would you understand that
I'm only a man

Dutifully, fulfilling your secret desires;
a candor so blatant, yet so smooth,
a co-miserer, a soul mate for life;
that's all I'm searching, all I am giving

        Tap-Tapping into my soul
        will you pay the price
Even if there was no charge
could you cover my back;
could you tell a lie,
could you be my story

> bard from par taken <

with the seas wailing of an irrelevant sadness
would you speak for me,
or would you demand my silence;
Should I become distant,

        Tap-Tapping into my soul
        can you be mine
A varying form of gray,
a sadness unbecoming,
a little kid on pun' due,
a shipwrecked void bombarded with rats

looking for an out
something I could let loose
a goal I've been wanting
a performance I can give. So

        Tap-Tapping into my soul
        searching for the shivers;
        Tap-Tapping into my soul
        drawing me to be near you;
        Tap-Tapping into my soul
        will you pay the price
        Tap-Tapping into my soul
        can you be mine
        even if the road is loaded.

                                                    <>

What is love?

Love is a gas
it feeds egos
and goes
where I can never go.
It is so far above you
that I can't even understand it.

Let me go beneath the Earth
and dwell
where love is given birth:
Allow me to drop a cell
and tell
one of all, you:

That I'd like to understand well;
not it.
But you.
Let me take a moment
to drop a subtle hint:
I like you.

<>

A home to come to

Holiday Season.
Recollecting at a time when most collect
      is not bad.
It makes me happy,
       filled with something I never had.

Your sad eyes   let me toss
Aside, all matters.
Inside   Me   (you & I)

This is whom I've become
since you came. Into my life,
a heart which knows not strife.

You're the best.
All others may rest,
but they can never sleep over.

You're for keeps.
I'm glad you didn't play,
       act for too long,
       or dance on that song.

How did you learn
A home to come to,
when none knew?
      the fires that burn
      my soul was not forced.

Upon a roof,

that concealed me from the truth,
No one ever said your name: Love.

<>

Serenity

If I drew
you: a picture
only bards can see

Would you cry?
the way the gods
opened up my heart,
the sky
under the Brooklyn Bridge

A canvas: oblique,
bare; drifting like the sordid past-
thundershowers at bay
illuminating the New York skyline,
lifting the stormy seas,
your soul

Is it so deep
or is the bay green,
murky, dark; a sadness
amidst such splendor and glory

Could we have mistaken
the view, the lightning and
the thunder for our theme song,
as if we were being courted,
serenaded by the heavens
to jump   into the splendor and glory.

A movie scene,

> guichard cadet <

it told of romanticism
of a broken lyricist
with a new bag. I
walked a mile-long journey
where denial and truth entwined
like a suicidal rope;

une histoire tragique,
two young lovers
on a different plane,

a level.
down where one
can touch but can never be

touched by your warmth,
caressed with your honesty,
the heavens applauded,
the sky took pictures,
and raindrops trickled

in a syncopated rhythm,
we toiled, trying to dig
deeper as if prying, but
actually reaching out

a friendly hand to touch
a soft ear to listen;
to my heartbeat:
outside was loud, but
inside there was…
serenity.

ND

In two
Conversations over the phone
you diagnosed
what others couldn't

pinpointed my nature.
Fences,

I lowered them.
A little
over three years ago,

I had never been hurt
but since then

I've become human;
thank you.

<>

My Guiding Light

My guiding light:
You question my blindness;
you try to steer me
from where I'm heading
perhaps if you step
to the side, and stop shining
in my face, cover my back, become
my shadow, you'll see the path I'm heading.

My guiding light:
A safe haven
where there'll be no cowering
into the forces that bind us.
A cave, a shelter open
not yet filled with the miseries of the past.

I know the moon's shine made love to you
then left you revolving.
Under the sun you basked, waving
gloriously, only to be burned,

I see, why you wish that
I worship the light.

My guiding light:
The darkness to which I yield
deference cannot be blanketed by the light.
The sun
I worship can spring a new start, but
first you must give me space;

> bard from par taken <

To create anew with you
by my side, covering
my back; shadows leaning against
one another
in a bleak landscape
man and woman who escape
the beaming light that only exposes
in order to negate
My guiding light.

<>

Picture Perfect Prose

If not a day in the life
then a month in a season
a chance to understand your pain and sorrows
or why your life is dubbed "sins of a thousand tomorrows."

If you need a focus or a reason
then accept this, and become my wife.

May the joys of today
erase the grief of yesteryears
while passion entwines our love
like the clouds in the sky above.

<>

At a loss for words

Another morning without you
finds me in the dark,
alone, scared,
screaming my insides out
because I'm falling
although there has been no letdown.

I am filled with fear,
some sort of abandonment
because I lack the understanding,
the words to measure how and why
this happens over and over,
with each time bringing a different twist.

I need you to be here
because "I'll keep it real with you"
I need to hear you say "I'm your baby"
not just tonight, but always;
I need to be able to come home from work
as the heavens tear and spill their joy,
and see you with your hair unkempt,
barefooted in your house clothes,
and your stomach swollen, carrying me forward.

<>

Moonlight at Dusk

Stranger things have happened.
We stood on the edge of forever
overlooking tomorrow
hoping today would never end.
Sorrow became the dawning of the night,
the cackling of a bird,
the strapping of a bra.

If we lived in stillness,
a canon couldn't have done us justice.

We were the pollen to be picked
the seeds to be planted
the bushes to be burned.
We were strangers in a foreign land
admiring the sights,
strolling the oft-traveled avenues of togetherness.
Until it came

Out of nowhere and tore us apart.
Me and you almost made somebody.

And you know what?
Stranger things have happened.

<>

Ma Soeur

Lately, I've been
hearing a silence
from your heart, nothing.

but from behind, your lips, anger;
perhaps
it is your daily routine,
you've got to exhale.

but what I am not
hearing. Is the happiness
perhaps; some of my thoughts:

The other night, when we were
alone – I wanted to

kiss! you
not in a sexual way, but
to let you know
I love
you. Like a sister

exhaling the positive.

<>

Fences

when you take one down,
you must realize
there's a limit

you then must be
willing to cross
over it. one limb

at a time
when barbed wires
is the barrier through

which we communicate.
our feelings have been muted
by that we should uphold.

<>

Moments of you in the Dark

Moments of you in the dark felt like a
    remembrance
    a pause of rationality, faith and sequence
    of a gleeful time where the truth was a lie.
    a whisper.
    a moan. It was like spitting into a tornado:
    solid disbursing liquid in an open space with little depth.

Moments of you in the dark became a
    reiteration
    a step into immaturity, compassion and lust
    of a gleeful time where the truth was a lie.
    a shout.
    a tear. It was like making the bed at night:
    gestures for the sort of court that leads to divorce court.

Moments of you in the dark ended in
    remorse
    a lost of cells, hope and morals
    of a gleeful time where the truth was a lie.
    a call.
    a smile. It was like a reborn cliché:
    two ships passing in the night (all night!).

I hope I stop having moments of you in the dark with others.

<>

Maybe We Should Walk Away

Last night was ugly;
Our fight played in my mind all day.
I found myself facing the computer
and not working on anything.

It seems that lately
We fight over the pettiest things.
To some couples that's a sign of care and concern,
but we were never like this.

You say one more try
But don't you realize
that love's not meant to be a war. <refrain>

II
I love you too much to see you suffer.
To see your eyes sad tears me up inside.
I know we have moments   moments of joy
but peaks and valleys has never been my style.

I hate coming home late
just to stay out of your way;
the love sessions without kisses
and those fights over the remote control.

III
This really isn't right
We are constantly fighting
I miss the getaway weekends   the snowball fights
and most of all I miss the warmth.

> bard from par taken <

To pretend there's anything left would be a shame;
So, let's remember the good times
The days when we first met,
and the first time I said I love you.

IV
To hold onto you would be so wrong;
it would make it seem as if we think our love's a game.
Don't go away mad; Do keep in touch;
Maybe being away may draw us closer.

I know you will miss me;
I'll miss you too
But trust me sweetheart,
You'll be better off without me.

<>

Vocals for Mo' Better Blues

Wishing you were here
Spending time with me

The times were not bad
yet we complained so much

I wish you were here.

II
I really miss your touch
and also your smile.

Can I call you soon
To reminisce a bit.

I wish you were here

Spending time with me

<>

society one: the unpaid extra

Untitled, Sexual Harassment

In. My house
there are several
rooms. The men know
all except the bedroom; the women
come
in all except the kitchen.
But there are other women
who don't come
at all, they think
I live
in a studio.

<>

The Unpaid Extra

You little bitch
with no tail
fixed from day one
wouldn't know to scratch it
even if you had the crabs.
You piece of shit

> *"Cut! Cut! look*
> *anger! anger, not cussing*
> *real anger. Show*
> *how I hurt you. ACTION!"*

Sadness becomes me
like black woolen slacks
shedding itself, after lying
packed near a white sweater, letting you know
the material you're made of,
how it feels to the skin

Skin has the ability to soothe,
keep warm, enliven the shape
the profile, the whole

life, as it is, is made to live

why do I feel such?
Simple: To live is life's verb form.

Your blank look
means I should expand

and spend time, my worth
even though I know
at this juncture, the very beginning, the preface
That my act, my poetic wisdom
will not even make the final cut
even if it is being taped,

No matter how live,
in your cutting room, I would
or could out-perform any of the stars
who will shine after I've helped you
            adjust the angles of the camera

But I will not make it.
I know you never promised me fame,
but all I wanted was an open mind
which would allow your lens to shed
if it were to brush against itself.

<>

An Ode to the Miscellaneous

Just Because
I was stone cold
Yet sensitive
you took me to be...

What you didn't
understand was that this
was my prerogative
and whatever you gave
I didn't take

'cause I knew
it would be poison.

Knew that behind
the smile and the words
there were blues
so sad that Bird
couldn't blow the horn;
melodies so deep
that Vaughn shouldn't
have been born
to make me keep.

To make me keep
My sense of truth
        dignity, and
        passion
as if it were a style
of fashion out of season,
and meat uncooked

because it was rare

To find a love
so private,
so kept.

You have to not only sing.
you must dance
before you can stand.

On your own two feet
is cute
but think of how lovely
I found you way back
when lunch was free,
and I thought I could launch

or spring
a start.

You had
enough class,
but I still don't
know your part

From the start,
part with the notions;
go with the motions.
Flow when Aunt Flow's
not on the go,
and champagne bursts
to quench the thirst
of one who could have been first

To taste the joy of almonds,
sing the song of Solomon

and jump into my arms.

To be there when the alarm sounds;
the bell to weather the storm
Of misery,
        history,
        and memories.

"Children!
Now, now children...play nice."

But chances are:
If we had set it off,
on the left
you would have stood
only temporarily.

Because all your contemporaries
(whether or not they bear the same name)
Wouldn't have lasted

Past twenty,
I would have fed them
to the sharks.
To the sharks baby!

                                              <>

Sweet Sweat

pouring over me
honey
but some odd reason it won't do
I shot thirty footers then some lay-ups
but for some odd reason
sweet sweat never came.
brought flowers
drank red wine
you know rosé with a rose.

Then a dose
of prose

I hoped.

surely you jest

Of course that wasn't my best.

I then set a test:
make her a pest
then say I must rest
'cause I want not go past the end.

No I jest not: The End.

<>

Kudos to Benito

For he was the one who ran across the field
ahead of me yelling.
He was the one who wanted it.
The one who didn't fear it.
The one who advanced;
the one who chanced death
to see if I'd been led under a false pretense.

To him: I give Kudos.
Because I was the one who,
melting under the sunshine
near the front of the gate
in the corn belt,
felt,
with assumption and simplicity,
that I too would farm
the cultivated fields of Farmer Buck
and Senorita Lucidity.

Because I was the one who,
driving from miles away
without seeing not even one coward,
continued forward hoping,
with assumption and simplicity,
that I too would farm
the cultivated fields of Farmer Buck
and Senorita Lucidity.

To him: I give Kudos.
For he was the one who faced
the enemy's hidden guns.

Guns loaded not only
with assumption and simplicity,
but with stupidity;
the one thing I, purposefully,
continuously,
gleefully
leave home without.

'twas a battle I could not have won.
Mercenaries of the third dimension firing:
   pellets without a cause,
   notes without legal tender,
   and stares without assignment
in a neutral zone
left an unpicked bone.
But Kudos to Benito,
my buddy,
who lays wounded like a shot pup
though alert like a hound:
for he was the one who turned stupidity into remorse
without uttering a sound.

<>

Mrs. Lowman: Birth of a Salesperson

After we kissed, I heard hissing
In the dark, I couldn't tell which one of us
Was the Snake
Out to make a Sale?

Saved?

II
Mrs. Lowman comes in all shapes
and sizes up the state
On the first date she opens the gate
then waits for the lyricist to sing the same old song
But if the dancer shows to part the legs,
She doesn't throw
she's no longer playing
the same old ho

"Hold on to your love"
Spirituality is her claim as she quotes scripture
to cling on gear one
after you've done scripted her
to the fast lane
as one who wanted to come
and get some because I'm a dove, pure from the start

even if I'm not looking for love!
"I really like you a lot"
If so, smile for me as in part the lips
whether you're short of breath,
speechless? dance baby dance
or at least I'll take a chance on the open palm.

III
As days passed, I found myself in an alley
where she threw a line to see if I knew
the time was of confusion, as if I were a mime.
with no voice, But
I had foreseen the revelation

"So Soon?"
As if time was to stand still,
small talk enabled us to grow closer
but to be real, she knew the deal

A joker is not a postcard
that you hang
on the wall,
await his call
then stall
because you think he's dull.

Pull
forward!
Step off,
Songstress

You have to regress
I ain't your best man;
I am better than that which can
            be there when you're the present.

Take a hike
"Do what you like."
I'm hurt.

IV

The dirt got in my eye.
I feel as if I've bought a bridge.
I'm hurt, you bitch!

Beanballs,
your protocol;
Thanks
for not answering my calls
after I smoothed the pit
and turned it
into a pot
where one can truly melt.

You salesperson
why do you edit
then try to get credit

for the writing on the wall
is for you. It's
the only state
in which you set a date!!

REAP!!

The grim
is not always slim.
"You know what I mean?"

<>

Segue or Sequel

Neither please
'cause I want not travel
for shame,
game,
or fame
the path from which I came.

in darkness, I received no light
though I made light of my intentions.

true: I am a character.
I'd rather be that than an actor
with not much factor
on why he's so cold.

FYI.
The hotter, the purer.
Coldness in some terms
brings germs
though not contagious, they're sickening.
They gnaw at you like rodents with braces.
Brace yourself sweetheart
The stroll has been designated to skip paces.
at two decibels
you I shall label
at point blank range
you I will stain
but in slow mo
'cause baby you must go
because I wants none.

> bard from par taken <

See? You do. I doesn't.
not even myself anymore
I can't return to a place
because you now want to learn
so you can save face
after I faced your ignoble stance
and commenced to dance
the waltz of statements false,
when in the beginning none was at fault
and such remained true 'til the end.
Now

Now
you want I to bend though it's over
backwards: I can't
fish not what I've ready hooked
can't put back what I never took.
Recall your book?

lots of empty pages
you asked me to write
one of the stages
the middle: I could not
For the beginning was but
a collection of novel ideas
with everything but characters
just actors and actresses.
Yes much like yourself.

Yes. I yearn for your caresses
and also
for rolls in your mattresses
But something's got to give:

If I choose to be a blind man
running to where he's never been,
you must become deaf,
dumb,
and wicked to the ways of man:
much like a queen.

It's weird that I found I saying:
"I'm never gonna dance again
            guilty feet have got no rhythm..."
Yeah I guess it is easy
to walk away and sing the hymn
but why dwell in the immaturity
the harmony,
the ceremony: that stupid ritual of yours
or its following.

a change must be made
a turn we must take
For continuation of completion is idolization of the past
            without care for the moment.

When if ever I plead guilty and say I do
look for a new walk of life
the next day: you I will jilt
without provocation
but fear of chance
that I will once again dance
the waltz of statements false.

<>

society two: the casual one(s)

Never More

It was a simple case of Miss Understanding.
Our bodies were entwined,
our eyes, moist with the remnants of sleep,
met like intersecting avenues,
the waves of an ocean when hitting the sand.

Around the table in its solid state,
burning under the high degree.
The freedom to merge
or to emerge into something new.

Our feet winced upon touch;
searching.
For a slight comfort;
for which there was nun.

She stood.
Her face, pale
despite the heat, she wore a black two piece
Her little legs, those of chicks,
strained at the toes;
the veins, green
the nails hovering, as if searching for worms.
Her mouth opened.
And her tongue hit her chin.

As she retracted it,
left a moist spot, as if she had sneezed.
The trail tailed off
near her thin lips, a mole.

> bard from par taken <

Her sudden bitterness flickered in my eyes
with the force of high voltage, as if it meant to harm.

I released
And she smiled.
Her teeth were perfect
(an admittance of been braced)
her breath warm, and inviting
spoke the words "never more…just enough"

And I've had.

<>

Guns of NeverHo

I had climbed higher
so I decided to go down
and climb again.
I had sunk low
but found this time
there was no need to sink.

I stood on top of Cloué Hill
a double barrel: My tool
and Decided this battle's
enemy need not be schooled.

Fortune rang
as the dread man sang
"Rag a muffin".
Jingles belled
when the saint yelled out
"Ho, Ho, Ho".

A full house with three queens,
and two jacks,
colors: black
both a spade
each with a club.
yes the deck was stack.

Partners in a previous ill-faded journey
became champions in a card tourney.
Stragglers in hollow halls
turned into pinups on grass-filled walls.

> bard from par taken <

One got caught cheating;
Another has not;
but all who played
got a fair shot
at targets who tried to duck
like unarmed warriors in an amusement park.

Before I reached the peak
I had to speak
like one who stumbled
into the fountain
while tippy toeing around the rim.
"This is not something I normally do
There has not been many
But there's been a few"

Just when I thought my chances
of firing were slim,
we danced the song that ended all dances:
"You gotta fast car…"

Incidental contact
sparked a chemical reaction
no foul was called
no flag thrown
So I retracted
as if I didn't own.
The lights came on
as the radio moaned
"What's the matter with your life"
A thought appeared
like a surprise quiz
it tested my being

> guichard cadet <

Am I really a member?

The fire alarm sounded
we must be burning

an explosion.
smoke filled the air
my comrade ran in,
like a trigger happy fool
drew his lethal weapon
gas around us.
I screamed
"Peace my brother.
This broad's for you."

His broad brow meant
who signaled
his slumped shoulders
who cares
If there's no war
why fire.

The sun shone.
as the box balanced 'tween three octaves
two pairs laid
like corpses in their graves.
Loaded my shot gun
in case there was an alarm at the gate
no one hailed
so I cleansed and headed for the next state.

We rode in on the high roads
like disciples out to spread the word

> bard from par taken <

bandits down to break the law.
Our quest paused
for there was no place else to go
in other words
we went back to see ones
we already saw.
Maria and Mary stood
took a look
and queried whether we'd been good.

Alone, comrade got found
to be a double agent
and came back to testify on my behalf
but I, NeverHo, smoothed it by self
said I spy for none
not even fun
I wait for the one

true
never blue
always merry
not afraid to marry
"sounds a bit scary"
yes darling
I wait
for you.

<>

Revenue Sharing

A hot bloody shrill
ran across the board
as if it had bonded
with a maverick bent on
merging.
As if the future
had no options,
only the liquid assets
stashed in a vault,
frozen.

Held at fault
'cause he dared bare
her bear skin
once tired of all the bull.

The crash came without warning,
and very little interest.
The acquisition, dull;
The takeover, bitter.
Secrets traded yielded junk,

for the moment had no treasure
and the mark hit
made no cents.

Express American sorrow
on the maturity of Seri's E's,
but limit the tears
in order to ease
the cease of our accountability.

The Casual One

A female live-human doll,
gets treated better than me?
How can it be that I am
Never. The chosen. has spurned
not my advances, but my promotion.

Everyone can know but
him. He's the other side.
Of this triangle, I once thought
it to be. Of equal sides
until I realized that I ask all

Of the questions: they begin
with Hypothetically

speaking in tongues. This broken
cypher. Similar to
island patois. Is your angle
Right? Therefore I have been

Wronged once again. Floating,
trying to avoid the needles,
your fingernails across my back,
the dinners you fix before you leave,
and after I've given you your fix,
to fix the rug you claim he can't cut.
Right?

Therefore I am. facing another
cold winter with gin,
as my lover. I do things

for you that I wouldn't do for my best

Friends! If I had
I would die. instead
I gladly accept this honor
that you bestow. Upon me:

Another.
At first it was assumed
By me: all of the time
You wear the visitor's jersey.
My home is your home; for,

According to you, you are
an illegal alien, yet you don't
want my green card? how
Come
Baby, come;
Come and share in the warmth
that only acute
thirty degree angles give.
My friends say to give you
everything except the boot
because I'm knocking the boots,
like a foot soldier kicking
knowledge to the youth:
<Don't walk over broken glass.>

My heart's never been;
in its place, my feet bleed.
For my pride and temporary joy,
is the fact that you are not mine.

> bard from par taken <

Yet I want you

To grow up in this vicious cycle,
and see. If you don't drown
in this blood that you have created,
I'll toast our union, save face
and let you wear white;
Hypothetically speaking!

Since I'm not home base, and
I bring you to soaring heights, yet
you claim to know what is right, and

I no longer want to serve
My function. has no limit,
hence never connect to the base.

Does that mean this figure really has
four sides with you playing
two, hopefully equal roles?
Or

Is this a line
a shark hooked onto
to teach this old man a lesson?

<>

In Control

If there is any such thing,
the only way to get it:

Deny Everything
when caught with your pants down
in the tower, always remember The Sun

Rose in the east and took a peak
at all. The relevant information,
there is none.

No facts to base. this charge
Deny Everything! go as far

To say that you never loved
Your mother? you tolerated her
After all,

she was the first.
to let you suck her breasts,
and to rub your balls.

before. They grow suspicious,
Knowing a cleaner is
a professional, specialist if I may,
Dog who tears slowly at human skin
for owners who agree to hide

his identity. a ruthless
glare that sparkles amidst bursts
of laughs garnered through intimate interstate calls

> bard from par taken <

leaving
wireless, breathless, inspirational
mementos in your box,
stains on your brain, and all
the while grabbing air, 'cause

Denial!! Denial!! you scream
Remember the time you giggled
at seventeen seconds before
your orgasms, minor notes
copping a plea for understanding

You beg: I want the truth

Never play the futures market
only 3% on the average win
It's a high risk business
To let a usual suspect spin a tale
Of forbidden intimacy while maintaining a distance
But the payoff is so great
If you get good at remaining in control,
By Denying Everything.

<>

Sufferah's Plea

Acknowledge me
for who I am, a kingdom can be built
an ocean can be circum
navigated by sharks, raked by green-eyed fishermen
polluted by novices
who can't swim? the red sea salty,
clean and refreshed is my vision
please take a bath, and cleanse the sins
Of the youth with a foresight, leaning back
against the deck
under the merciless sun, we sweat. our toils
unappreciated; our women
left us to.
fend for ourselves, create our own
illusions of the believers
got the serpent under the rainbow
burning hot under the collar – shit
"just make me wanna holler";
gaiety has never been my state,
for I could never. debate the wanting
the fear, the quickness of our willingness
to make friends, I lose
my sexuality, a random act, a blatant hypocrisy?
True. But my form should be the norm;
you should cheer for me.
You should acknowledge,
better yet recognize that a false reading
of a conjurer's tale leaves noses bloody.
unable to leak I spray
Salt on the wound
a blindfold on the crack

> bard from par taken <

Of your eyes, they're pretty
a darkness which shines to cover the light
they lock me so tight   I feel
for you there's nothing I would not do;
for I would stop.
I would come into the space
welcome the Black back
admit the beauty of life
the clear waters, the comforting nature of the waves
the tasty cod you have offered
Shame no more
I feel for you.

<>

City Island Blues

Moving. Further away from
The truth: I can't handle it,
this feeling which leaves me
so empty because it does belong to me.

Seated. Facing a polluted landscape
where two industrial chimneys blew
Smoke(d)
not far from the Throgs Neck, I felt
a beak reach its peak as it darted
up and down on my neck.

Were I one to romanticize the truth,
I would have gladly debated the view;
how can one not visualize and beautify
the smoke flowing in the atmosphere
climbing the ladder of a sparsely lit gray sky,
few stars twinkling, and me wondering

If I had been a slave
would I have broken North
or would I have been one lulled
into a quiet passionate somber like that

Of a sunny early spring weekend
where Blacks danced in a mountainous region;
As if they had reached their peak, they glowed
like happy campers perched, on a boulder
in a poisonous bush.

And once bitten, they naturally became;

> bard from par taken <

but before acknowledging the sting, they marveled
at the energy, the mental heat
being dispensed for a cold woman's shower;
the tears flowed, not from the eyes
but the brow sweated, revealing the anger

Of having swallowed a bitter pill, I
Coiled, recalling that I too can be a snake;
to wrap myself around your neck like a true sneak,
suck your breasts to spew this venom

you call the truth: This
lingering to a morbid past,
this done deal – what transpired between us?

For shame be me, "I pity the fool";
But irregardless of my unwillingness
To shoulder this load, I feel
you should know that you have not a clue

As to what is what, even if
"Everything is Everything"
"You can call me crazy."

But you will soon
see that you are just
another chimney blowing smoke.

<>

By the fireplace

I had the dream
Then I didn't
know that captain's log?
"No, but it's stardate tomorrow."
My penis oily, still dripping
the last bit hit under your navel

Why did I pull out
to leave your gut
scarred, like a windshield hit with bird shit
I can't come visit
someone revoked my ghetto pass
or maybe I know that captain's log.

Stardate: The Blizzard,
the excuses, the reasons you didn't visit
the hints, hoping that my logic

would tell that I was the tail
but when attached to an attache,
women ain't so nice
some nègre has to pay the price
'cause gentleman soil women who shoot dice
without knowing that captain's log.

<>

Heaven and Hell

As time goes by
slowly as fine wine ages.
Ours is a love for the ages,
and only the sages will understand.

Why it is I froze, looking
up at the ceiling, long enough
for you to ponder

what's on my mind
The 2 things you said:
lack of trust, and
you can't pretend a year didn't go by

That alone made it reality.
To know that the glee
of you and me is only temporary;
that I can't have you

How I want. for you
to be free, not only for me;
for you are the world.
the reason I had to freeze
and cork my passion
and spill my seed while french-kissing.

I long for you
So much, that it is scary;
I may trust but I still fear

To be taken for granted;

Once more to bite my lip
and swallow my tears
as another new lover learns
because my soul burned

In the fire called Experience,
I'm a teacher who watches bright pupils
return
to make their peace, they shed.
turn the good into stress
and deny I was the best they ever had.

I can't promise that I can
continue to hide my vulnerability;
yes! I may cry and cuss

not just for sympathy
but for the understanding that I need.

<>

Fahrenheit

I'm back
But it's actually my first time
here.

We acknowledged that
Passed over twice,
we should have done
what TLC said, and creeped

A long time ago
when it was 90 degrees outside.
I felt so right with you
didn't fret when I idolized
to see the smile, the eyes

openly touch you, but
Now I wink and try to decipher
your apprehensiveness

I'm not sure
if it's hotter
or was last night the spring

The heat means I'm inside
But I never knew
A fever meant we've come

full circle? I
must have missed something

<>

Friends!

Just when I thought
I had love figured

out!

But then I found myself
Back

In. Always thought you
played the periphery, like a jilted lover
or a laid-off postal worker

waiting for the moment
to come. to slap me in the face
while I was not looking,
you heard me say that you were
in love

with me, there was no doubt.
It couldn't be love
even when you slapped me
with the letter

"No it can't be!"

Good, it isn't because we were not
Cohabiting
yet 200 miles away,

I opened the envelope, and it slapped me.

> bard from par taken <

Hit me so hard, I almost
Called the hotline, but then I heard
"That's what friends are for..."

<>

Dogged by Dogma

Laying in the coma,
my bed is filled
with sorrow, I lay
alone

not necessarily. waiting
for the one, my soul mate
but I've come

to realize there are
four senses
programmed
years after birth,
a chip in our brain
implanted,
converted to androids,

machines in human form
that can only break
free if individuality is claimed.

As a joke
She & I, two strangers were introduced
both previously unaware of the other's existence,
and clueless to our individuality,

how the switch is a feeling.
turned on, we would
go insane,
useless to ourselves, but
Key to the continuity

> bard from par taken <

of the collective, the dominion.
the pursuit of happiness
can be found easily unless

one sense comes into play.
We can be deaf, dumb, blind
but heartless, we fail

to realize the strength.
of conforming, we understand;
of rebellion, it's a trend;
being alone is unacceptable

but programmed so well,
She turns me off by asking
"What will they do without you?"

<>

Crutching the Crushed

An axe fell near.
At first I thought it got my ear
then I heard not a word
but a herd of would have been targets
crying like maggots
that had been seduced then left.

They came to my side
        said they'd bare the red cross;
thus wear the badge of courage.
They tried but couldn't because:
        they left their crutch in storage.
        their insecurities they wouldn't toss.
yet they claimed they felt my pain inside.

I'm hurt 'cause I've been fooled
not because I am.
I am in mourning 'cause I awoke this morning
without blush in my cheek
        dough in the oven
        nor corpse in the coffin
which means I was either the meek or weak.
To a lost person I must have spoken.

Why? 'cause I awoke
without blush in my cheek
        dough in the oven
        nor corpse in the coffin.

I usually kill or get killed.
My aim's not to maim, tame or shame.

> bard from par taken <

This is not a game.
I never promised fame.
Come back! I said come back
damn it, for I you have maimed, tamed and shamed.
Come back because I killed you.
Come back and put
blush in my cheek
dough in the oven
and corpse in the coffin
like all the others who spend life
crutching the crushed.
Come back

<>

Barred

Trapped
in a cocoon
Old Gold down
wondering – why?

is it the thing
that one fears most
she gives out?

Have not heard
from you. I got another

someone took your lunch
money,
kept me at bay

because you feared,

I cried when I opened the box

and found it
empty:
No treasure. to fill
my pleasure; Nothing

to hold on to you
would be romantic, but
how would it look: to see
an old man by the sea
jocking immature,

> bard from par taken <

candid – I can no longer be;
I've been...
barred.

<>

May Day

May day; May day...
I've lost all control
I'm plunging at thirty thousand feet
May day; May day...
Any body...

May day be bright;
For the night was bleak.
Of passion, and lost I speak.
May day help me find the light.

Whether it be the glory of the times had,
or the dreams of situation wanted;
the breath of cold children escaping
while they trek the snow, on way to school
with the winds gusting their backs,
and tossing their scarves from shoulder to;
the flakes stinging playfully on their cheeks. Let it be

Let it be summer. Let it be
Somewhere; anywhere.
Let it be.

The bare branches,
the cloudy sky,
a window of a brownstone that is open
ever so slightly, the breeze of whispers heard,
squeezes felt.
The curling under knitted blankets,
the damp locks hanging over trimmed brows. Let it be

> bard from par taken <

Let it be spring. Let it be
Something; anything.
Let it be.

The even days,
the gloomy nights,
with few stars shining bright.
The indecisiveness,
of questioned associates,
and mistakes uttered.

The frozen stares,
wondering if anyone's there
awaiting the arrival,
avoiding the fall.

The anticipated calls,
the pretender stalls,
and the offended rings,
not once, but over and over.

Again I feel the shift;
again I feel the slight.

The precious stones are belted.
By the warm water of cold days,
    we stay and bathe in gin.
Again and again.

The children are now grown,
    and I am left alone.
To Despair's child,
    I should have never shown.

> guichard cadet <

My face is a constant reminder
   of a deed undone,
   and a mission blown;
My smile, a question mark
   as to who bested whom,
   and should we try
Again and again and again and...

<>

a farewell to art & addiction

Untitled, shallow

I use to write
sad poems because
Art meant misery.

Thought I was
dipping deep
until I realized how
easily things affected me.

<>

A hug will do

Little Arthur cried
'cause Art was going out the door.
simply walking out of his life.

Cried because, to Art,
he will become a lost soul
though bold
(matter of fact the coldest)
from hence, the mold broken.
Will never wear gold as a token
Will thus chase the sole
to find a solid firm.

Something to hold in the night,
when we stare
<how dare we stare?>
As if we hadn't gotten a look.
You know, of that blank verse
with no space, just holes
which other losers.

Others: you mean I'm not the first.
To rehearse, as if I'd started
blank verse.

To create on a clean slate,
as if I were once a pauper
and can actually act proper,
    no radical shifts
    no need to uplift,
    or teach.

I may have done that,
but Yo, I never bleach

Colors: the tide wasn't
your cousin. The brother died
without a frown, just tears.
mine, and yours
can never make up a front
so milky as that of the way.

we stood on the hill, looking at the vacuum
          sensing the darkness,
          trying our darndest
          to be a captured.

As I belong, I realize
that Little Arthur is dangerous
because of not his blindness,
but his insistence that perception's path is wide.

Between you and me: he had to
because all Art said was
a hug will do.

<>

Pleasure Bay

Whisk me away.
let I bathe
as if Pleasure was truly by bay
I know it isn't today
but let's pretend
yes. for me
who else could light the candle
near the fireplace
fill you as if you are really Space
& not just a face
I visit when I leave home
base(d).

Yes. I
never knew it would be this strange
or else I would have danced sooner.
Never thought I was a late bloomer
'cause I always advanced
Yes. They
used to call me a prodigy
a blue monkey's effigy
a cartel of charm
with a void near his left arm,
a cavity in his chest.

Always thought I was smooth
you know
Flow with the groove
but I now realize
from the twinkle in your eyes
that I scathe the pit.

97

Why such an intrusion?
In my own confusion,

A state of fate without date
just wait.
I express agony,
harmony,
as if an instrument had been played.
I'm either on the roof
of my own cloud
or I've been laid to rest
like a pauper

frozen.
unable to catch a quarter.
note
the empathy. the realization
of a new dimension
a towering ascension
a fog surpassed,
an enemy stomped
but still grasping for straw

'cause I'm scared to get this deep
because I scathe
when I bathe at bay
in Pleasure Bay.

<>

Death is Legal

Abortion. War or
Should I say bout
with the bottle.
Alcohol. Guns or
Should I say fire away.
Wheat and Barley
for those who start early
or take the train at night
in spite of class
in the morning.

Well hung until it was over.
Stumbled into a fly nightstand
who called me lover.
Bum. Druggie.
call me what you like
'cause I'm going to the high
wearing a tie
investing more than a G
at the U.

Peasants in the valley hoping
for comfort.
Can't get blessed, though it's death.
Little girls shuffling uneasily,
it's time for gin.

or Cisco. Liquid Crack!!!
no pun intended
Standing on line isn't good for you, though it's death
D runk **W** omen **I** ncite

Or should I say **I** ndict.
Abide. Stomach. Legal
Homicide. Suicide.
No need to hide
Since Death is Legal

<>

Raw Talent

He drives
to the base line.
pumps once,
then a shoulder fake

puts up the shot.
to brake
the morale.
the canal,
the corral
takes the shot
to break

the tie on which we lie,
the dread we bred
the reason why:
we bled.
The chance to take

a shot at the base line?

<>

Cool Guy, Run

A paradox of fortune
lent me a sense
at first it bounced slowly.
for, shame be me,
I was unused to it.
I wondered daily while wandering nightly.
It now beats furiously
but still appreciate that it bounces.
here and there?
Yes. Scared of nowhere: yes.
I must run
'cause it chases,
as if it is on hunt
Yes. I tried
but it won't;
just gives blunt answers
when I am depressed
and shots to make me a dancer.

Still: I once posed.
Still I run, because
A pause in wonder forces the senses to wander
        after pondering why I no longer want to be a wonder.

<>

> bard from par taken <

Withdrawal

part too
I can't
not after learning I never came.
Just went
to the store
to get more and store it
in evil's body.
it never had definition
but now it has color

      Eyes or skin   must be glass
      (as in looking)
      <just a thought>

Kill me
for the pain is too much
to bear.
it makes me bare
not the physical
but the aspect I never felt

      just thought about
      <just a sight>

beyond myself
I can't see
the purpose of knowledge.
no one wants one
to create
as if life imitates Art

> guichard cadet <

Is imitation leading on
just to one day create
<just a feeling>

I don't respect abstract creations unless
they're absurd

change like seasons
confuse like nature
control through perception
thereby enabling you to know
One: me
All: you & me

<>

Si Dieu Veux

Many
May Not Know
This: all I ever had
was my faith in God. Never
feigned Understanding nor Knowledge

Only respect. those
who've come before us,
curse us
with their faint whispers
and teary eyes
thinking they know

What we have become:
potheads galloping through
unwashed maidens with dirty toes.
with lack of a better pose,
I grab my crotch.
I'm bad, will smoke, send

a soul searching, continually
breathing because I realize
the cycle is vicious
only because some claim
to understand and know
my faith (or lack of).

<>

YMG

I am
because I'm
young, mobile and gifted.

because I've been lifted
from under the microscope,
and cleansed of the stain
which will never the Less
remain
within my coffin
confined as my past,
my best.

Young is the eager eye
that pins skeptics on the spot
and bequeath them to stand
on their doubts.

Mobile is the motive of a nomad
who realizes that he is mad
and is content to be
because he's never had.

Gifted is the next breath;
the continuity,
the progress,
the self.

II
YMG is a spiritual.
look at God

from a believer's angle:

It is the joy
of a boy
who became a con's toy
the day after he landed
in the can.

It is the laughter
of swingers with surnames Beaux.
Elizabeth and Leslie,
Two sisters with no mass
who cross brothers,
don't deal with others,
and stand like flowers without a vase.

It is the appreciation of paths not taken;
'roads not crossed.
It is: what it is.

<>

What people do

He's trying to be…

I knew he was
that type
who goes searching
for a life
in order to hype,
and be with
those who go
to know
their limits

II
Are Boundless
Sombers
the fall of the empire
or the umpires
who call
a ball
in order to strike
a match
and watch

The phoenix burn
in Pseudonym's land

Oh no!
Not him
Two

Not them also

III
We were all
Good folks who
Knew jokes
commonly

new jokes

But if you step
sideways.

Take another space
and face
a new challenge

<The Boundless Sombers sense a change>

Everyone does it
yet
"They wanna make you think it's a black thing
        or a crack thing…"

<Don't, they say!>
Just hope
for the day
when some more
will know the score
is a tie,
and that the war
is an understanding
none understands!

IV
Don't down yourself!
if you were holy,
you'd be full of holes

Like me
or diss me
Don't miss
because I refuse
to be your mister

and hold your frame

.

then realize
I missed her.

I can't catch curve balls
or match
colors, and mood shifts
but I can pitch
a bitch
so high
just for you
to call a strike
and point at the one
you don't like

Then call it me.

Didn't mean to
throw you a fastball.

I don't believe

> bard from par taken <

in learning curves.

I'm new at this;

Are you a swinger?
If so, recant
my name; but
remember the game:

V
On one we press
        the gas.
At neutral,
        we see who has an ego
        at level zero.

In the dark,
I didn't want to

But I had to blow a leaf
in order to get a life.

Don't love me!
This is what people do
to be true to themselves,
to be zero.

<>

SlowFoot's Code:
turning stills in a stall into stirrers

Sensitivity

I remember
As a child, I
use to cry easily

Was most sensitive
but then I graduated.
into manhood, I
brought a lot of notions
and bought others.

It's not the women;
nor is it the men;
nothing complex
just layers

Of indifference.
not towards humanity in general,
but myself.

The personal hurt reaches
The whole if one is not
allowed
to ever stand alone.

<>

The Sick Parable

I cough daily
I wash under my arms yearly
but I always keep my charm
It's tough!
But it's a must.

If ever I bathe
consider me sick
If ever I brush
call me a lush
If ever I comb
lead me to my tomb
after hitting me with a brick
but pray: for my soul you must save.

I nurture the fears of other men
as if there were my own
Call me a soldier: for I have killed
for fun.
Call me a martyr: for I will die
under the sun.
Call me a rebel: for I live
by the gun.

If ever you see blood on the path I pave
consider me sick
If ever you see blood on my skull
call me a lush
If ever you see blood on your hands
lead me to my tomb
after hitting me with a brick

> bard from par taken <

but pray: for my soul you must save.

I cry all the time wishing you were mine to mold
or had my mind to hold
for a short period
so you too could feel
the sickness others call unreal.

<>

Young Nation on the Rise

It's time for us
to have our own
Fuck the Old
Black
and White.

Let's have
a little color.

<>

Why We Die

We die,
Unlike an aged star

Our cries loud.
Corpses bleeding
reincarnated spirits
are we

Survivors they say;
Sufferers we are

taught to face
the hardships we endure
to save face
we accept

humiliation:
it's just a test

detested! we cry
just to bring a smile
we jest.

<>

Peace

Peace is a disease.
It tears you two pieces.
Choose one, you'll always
have the other with you. Only as a thought!

What if all mankind had a common belief?
    Life would be fictional
    We'd be actors forming our character
    From the given script. A ship
        sailing near the horizon,
        seeing day's break,
        sensing the sun has already risen.

If so, what worse ship?
    None except that of the Past,
    When the population wasn't dense.
    And none danced in the fog
    of Cloudy Sky!

Man with wings?
    Yeah, you'll be alright.
<'cause you're not now>
Because Today does not wait
For Tomorrow will never come.

You must go to the risen sun,
And from the present, go fa'ther
because peace has already begun.

<>

118

The Bridge

Don't try to cross
Universal's Bridge
Unless,
you are willing
to walk a personal's plank
into the depths of the See.

Perceivers
focus on the dots
of the loc's

Tic Toc
Tic Toc

If you Vanish,
they will tarnish
the strength of the pond.
To them: it was too small
                to fall into,
                and narrow enough for you to crawl out of.

Yet none of them ever borrowed
        a piece to scrawl
        the call of two,
        to seal your broken skull.

<>

What is the future?

What's held in the brain
of dreamers? a gas
that passes for the mind

Is actually mine what's been broken
or do we lay
in trivial pursuit
or should we cling to the past

"Which has been established?"

A question spewing out of the mouth,
rapid in eagerness yet incongruous,
like the air up there.
Seemingly from the norm, a drunkard who cheers
after a hard workday for which

There's no compensation from the concrete.
for the solid realizes
the fluidity of dreamers
but only acknowledges the willingness to become.

of liquid, we have no qualms
for calmness can be us
as well as the rapid, volatile rush

To freeze. At 32 degrees Fahrenheit

<>

Flagrant

Why has?
Passion become the observed
holiday of lost souls
whose bodies challenge the mind's rule.

Only a fool?
Stands a chance
with the media peeking,
and the government seeking.

Our private lives?
Desperately need to part
From the puppeteers' strange request
and the puppets' act of control

The self?
Has beens
Stored on a shelf
right by the rice and beans.

Stake not your mind?
Unless you're willing
To cut the strings
and drop.

First Face?
Broken glass, the fact
rebellion of the lax
has us going back.

To rhyme?

Flow on time then end
thus pretend
All is fine.

As wine?
Goes down well
Please do tell
All.

Who answers the call?
We live in hell.

<>

Aren't You Proud?

"There's a war going on across the sea.
Brave soldiers killing the elderly.
Whatever happened to unity..." Run DMC

Dagger in my hand
"I wear the badge of the land"
A shattered mind is my weapon
My broken heart's the reason.

I cry in the day
'cause at night I stalk.
The harsh pavements of reality is my walk.
And of this I talk.

On our planet
there's too much strife.
"Fuck my wife, take my life."

In my neighborhood
there are prudes
and local hoods
whose favorite phrases start, "I could".

Up the block
beggars block my path,
my boat they rock,
and my jock they ride.
"Where's the other side?"

Across town
two slain...

the whole city's in pain…
"at 4 a.m. don't take the train."

In the street
we meet
as the cops beat
"what a team: your buns; their meat."

Down the highway
Five-O thinks freeze
'cause my ride's large
and I do as I please.

At home Johnny smokes cess
while lil sis lays rabbit to rest
in peace mother hits the pipe
father's not there.
"He must know Bess."
My. Her son

<>

Slowfoot's Code

<into the self>

The adverse effect
    of the rising sun,
    which is such
    only because of dusk.
    The moon,
    ever so disobedient
    yet conforming
    with sequential tides,
    shining proudly
    on his knightly excursions
        of pride,
        fortitude
        and his might (i.e. maybe)

It is true
    that the drops
    are eternally embedded
    on our stones
    as the hearts of our cause.

No matter how just,
    we must test
    each plus.
We cherish not
    only the deeds done,
    those who have gone,
    the broken's bone;
    But also the one
    Left alone to dwell

in his own private hell:

The First.
Farmer,
The cultivator of crops
The seed
Invisible, the present.

Second.
Too None,
The dedicator
Shadow, the current.

The Third.
Know Ledge,
Fame deShame
Badge, the pastor.

Fourth.
Warrior
The symbol
Soul, the swimmer.

Fifth.
Carpenter,
Misfit, the tester
sinister,
The Swinger
The Chameleon,

FLIPSIDE, A BEING
A character, A planter
A dot

within a shell   at first
then
as if
Harvest time
an eye, a vision.
pulse.

Nurtured.
The eyes cleansed daily,
as if the pupils were pearls.
Nightly.
A simple question
      "What did you see today?"

The only test:
      That of the five
      senses, the changes
      of influence.

Swing
The pendulum back to place;
Let not Blossom bloom,
for Doom has not
touch the spot.

Socially.
Use only The Common Tenth: your mind
Part your smallest piece
To the letter,
to none's pattern;
make up your own mind.

Load it

> guichard cadet <

Build
divide

Upon it
bestow your inner self.
<no line should be thinner>
for it is only Space
a Vacant Lot

P.S.   *"Corruption of the mind is worse than that of the soul."*

Back!

Miracle workers
somehow performed
a smooth   transition;
forced you to move
one over,
when there was but one.
You

If you are walking
under water, and
the other flows.
Fly off the handle.

If you are allowed,
I hope you can flow
Because
"we all float down here"

Level Zero.
Skeezers come through

> bard from par taken <

Automatic weapons:
            seize fire.
About face
Wipe your brow
you are now

Visionaries.
plot the progress
set the course.
You've already rehearsed
the scenes with the hearse
            and the ho'rse.
It's time
To use force.

Control the revolver.
Instead of BIGGER
pull the trigger.

Terrorize the dome:
Protect your home.
Solve

Not social
But the spiritual

Inequality:
The superior's personal state
            which allows the collection
            to equate a common swing.
A step toward
            Doom: forever's shine,
            or the drift

Survival of the fittest?
        should not depend on the destruction of the shittiest,
        or on the whims of the pettiest.

Currently,
Both.
It's time to swing   "Swing Batter Swing!!"

                                                     <>

Learn to say I love you

For the pain
and the suffering it has
brought us. to a place
where if we are able to say it
to our mates
just to ejaculate
or reach that orgasmic state
we should look at whiteys and
learn to say I love you.

Behind the facades
and the charades; of our covert
spook by the door tricks,
by the essence of our depression.
The only history we need

to remember, or better yet
realize that the whites must have
told our ancestors
"I love you."

Why else can't we
allow our hearts to turn to stone
to match the bone
in its most erect state, while embracing
the co-ed who a decade ago
in our senior year kept us at bay,
alone to grease our palms
while reading psalms.

II

Where there is love, there's hate,
so close, peering
like a stalker

with a revolver, you can't start
for your heart's too soft,
drained like a tomato squeezed whole,

to flavor the meat, you recite `
the antidote of an imaginary revolt.
Hate is lonely, love doesn't want to be near it.

But hate follows,
like a spurned lover it swallows
the bold face lies,
the meal shared with other lovers
sitting across cafeteria tables trying

to be friendly, a hug
to a strange white say it
GET CLOSE
GAIN TRUST
don't grease shit
Hit it hard
from the back

and as tears roll
like beheaded peasants
say...I love you.

<>

Untitled, Misery

Evil stares penetrate the wind
the closet swings open
to bury the living,
heads nod to undecodable rhythms

the lock clicks to
the left are sly peeks.
the right mouths with no tongue

in explicable jargon we simmer.
While the swimmer boils in the blood
the tide floods the trapped
in lagoons
dirty
muddy
and blue.
we witness the regression in its truest form.

Blind man run
but we can't catch up;
it's like catch-22
(so to speak)
but we can't fathom
or even interpret the path.

Children smile so stupidly;
doubting Thomas isn't for me,
he's a part of the conspiracy
even though he knows the plan.

The time cannot be told,

for the day ahead is steeper than a Hill.
Smile little girl
Wink little boy

In four years, we will
not see the revelation;
but in two blank blacks we will feel...
Misery.

Upon us like a burn
from a turf.
the scab voted for the ticket;
once resolved, now absorbed.
In the closet, two shook
the hanger, then a lever.

one felt the draft
but none sensed the misery.

Please help!
this bleeding child
will not die.
He will waste, up until
the very last, the transfusion.

Oh my, cry for the
brave soldiers deserted in the sand

Of time I speak,
do you see
do you see
can't you feel the misery.

"Sister. Sister"
pardon me for this intrusion
Officer,
but what's the meaning of blue
when it is so cloudy outside,
and the inner-self so dark?

Orphans
"I count down here to thee"
begging for the span
pleading for notice
in this bliss
in this bliss
I see only the fake
smiles
of beggars
bound to the

Others
can you sense the tense

Past
why don't you part
since you won't be a
breath of hope
a signal for lost ships

Bounty
Oh Glory
from years ago
to
today

> guichard cadet <

to instill
(or better yet)
reinforce a stain almost vanquished

Oh Glory:
Many want to see you burn
in the fires of Pseudonym
Get what I mean?
"Burn, Motherfucker, Burn!"

From the window,
I can see a whole squadron
of ashy feet running
in chains
with links from one arm
to the ankles
shot
guns
in the other
blowing
violent
the wind
the beat, syncopated

Shattered
The visual effect.
Tears from a five year old
burned by an iron
which her mother uses
to bake the mind

To bring the bread
she cocks open

> bard from par taken <

while Mad Man
Rooster's
Blunt objects to the Ghost.
but for most
the pipe is not an escape,
but a cage
for birds who can

Fly like vagrants reaching for a quarter of approval,
I nod and shed a tear;
For an escape, I pitch
and make a friend
a fiend, an enemy.

Be gone my holy child
the fears of yesteryears are now the tense.
Present yourself if you indeed are apart,
but don't fool
life's too cold, too
gray, too conspiratorial, too
filled with misery.

Be gone…

<>

Angst Anger: in stills

The fireplace behooves at the dawning of day.
a leaf whispers to its neighbor through chilling
stems
which stems from a night.
unprotected from frost
dew to suffer a chilling winter
a breeze of melancholy beckons glory to the forefront.
wood crinkling comme pommes de terre qui fris
heaven awaits as the fire rushes
sparkles light the bear's skin
while
flames search the bare skin.
Inhabitancy is its nicked.
revelation: the message.
A chorus of little happy feet stumbling unscrupulously
the parquet floor whimpering, unable to summon help
As the seconds tick and the seasons switch,
the helplessness scourges the leaf.

<>

About the Author

Guichard Cadet was born in Haiti. He moved to New York in 1977, and received his bachelor's degree from the State University, College at New Paltz. He is a member of Kappa Alpha Psi Fraternity, Inc.

Guichard has been a participant in the Caribbean Writers Summer Institute, and has a MBA from Howard University. He is the founder of La Caille Nous Publishing Company.